How to Draw
ANIMAL FRIENDS

Learn to draw 20 amazing animals,
step by easy step, shape by simple shape!

Illustrated by Peter Mueller

Getting Started

When you look closely at the drawings in this book, you'll notice that they're made up of basic shapes, such as circles, triangles, and rectangles. To draw all your top animal friends, just start with simple shapes as you see here. It's easy and fun!

Circles
are used to
draw a standing
dog's chest
and hips.

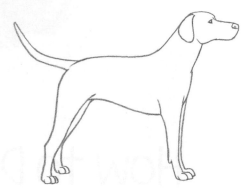

Ovals
are good for
starting out
almost any kind
of fish!

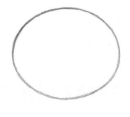

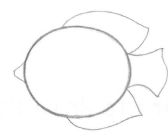

Triangles
are best for
angled parts,
like a
snake's
head.

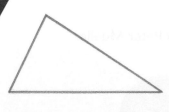

Tips

There's more than one way to bring your pet pals to life on paper—you can use crayons, markers, or pencils. Just be sure you have plenty of natural hues: black, brown, and white, plus yellow, orange, and red.

Pencils

Crayons

Markers

Puppy

This lovable Lab is still a youngster, so it has a chubby body. Begin with an oval for the tummy and a circle for the head.

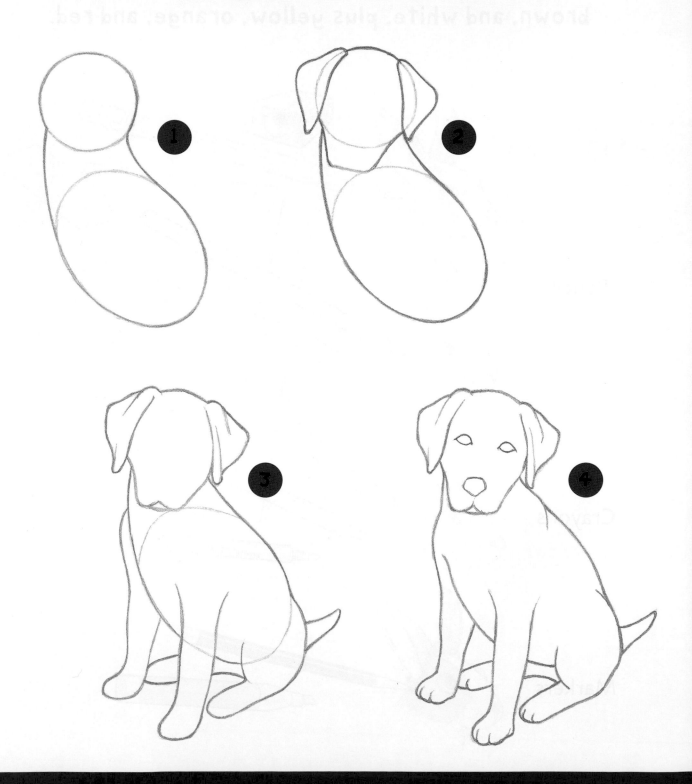

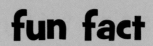

Kitten

5

6

fun fact
Even puppies who are "free to a good home" need care and upkeep—and that takes cash.

Kitten

This tiny tabby has a fluffy body and short, thick legs. Its round eyes and triangular ears look huge on its little furry frame!

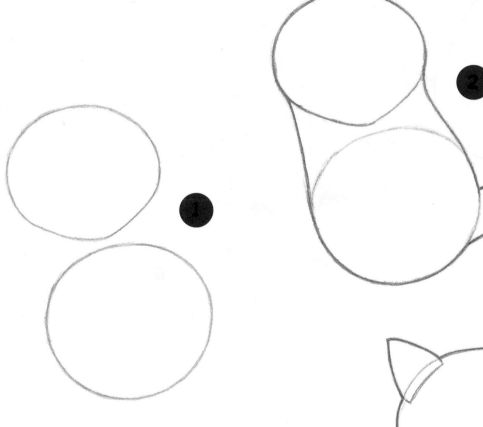

fun fact

Cats have excellent hearing and very flexible ears! They have 30 outer-ear muscles that rotate each ear a full 180 degrees. This means felines can hear in all directions without moving their heads, which helps them pinpoint where sounds are coming from.

Betta

Male Siamese fighting fish are known for their large, beautiful fins, which they proudly display when they meet another male fish!

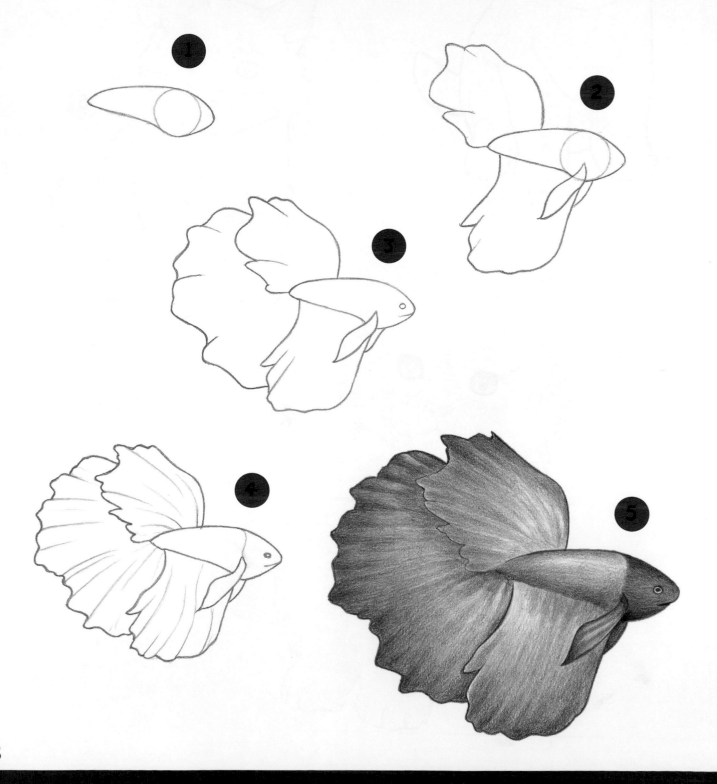

Cockatiel

The cockatiel's crown of feathers stands up when the bird is excited, but it lies flat and curls at the end when the bird is calm.

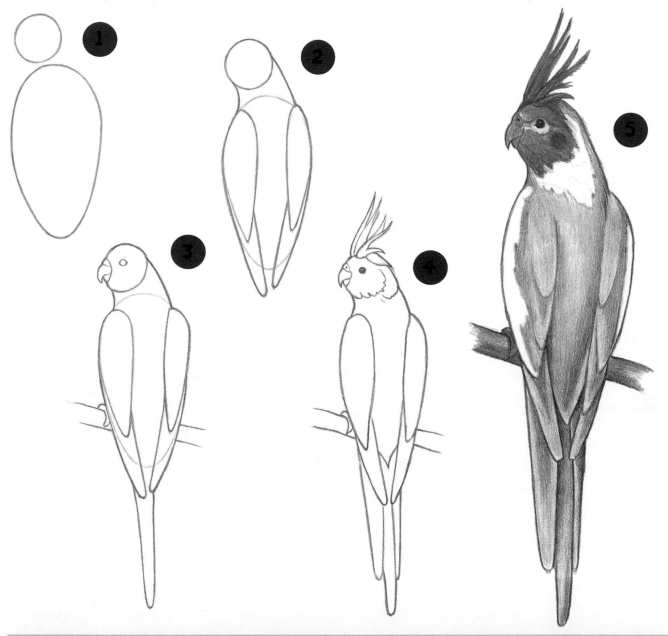

fun fact

Because it's a social bird, your cockatiel might enjoy having a pet of its own! Experts say canaries make good pets for cockatiels. But don't expect your 'tiel to take care of the canary's feeding and cleanup; those will be your responsibilities!

Bunny

This Lop-eared rabbit's body is round, but it isn't a perfect circle. Its long ears droop down, but its short tail swoops up!

fun fact

It's not unusual for caretakers to discover their pet bunnies fast asleep. After all, rabbits are nocturnal, which means they're active at night, so they sleep during the day. And, on average, rabbits take 16 naps per day to get in a full 8 hours of sleep!

Frog

It isn't easy being green! This amphibian has a few unusual features, like legs that fold and eyes that sit on top of its head!

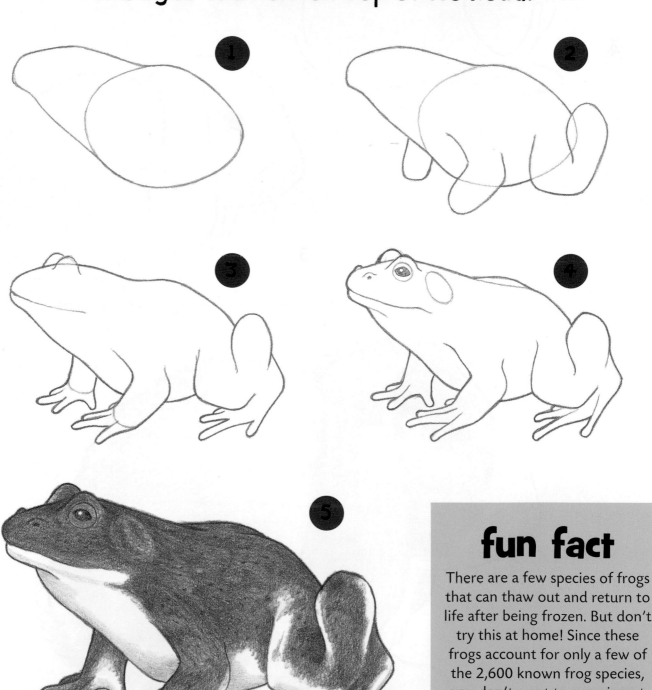

fun fact

There are a few species of frogs that can thaw out and return to life after being frozen. But don't try this at home! Since these frogs account for only a few of the 2,600 known frog species, you don't want to experiment on your hip-hopper!

Mouse

This little mammal has tiny rodent
features: small, round eyes; a tiny pink nose;
a long, thin tail; and itty, bitty toenails!

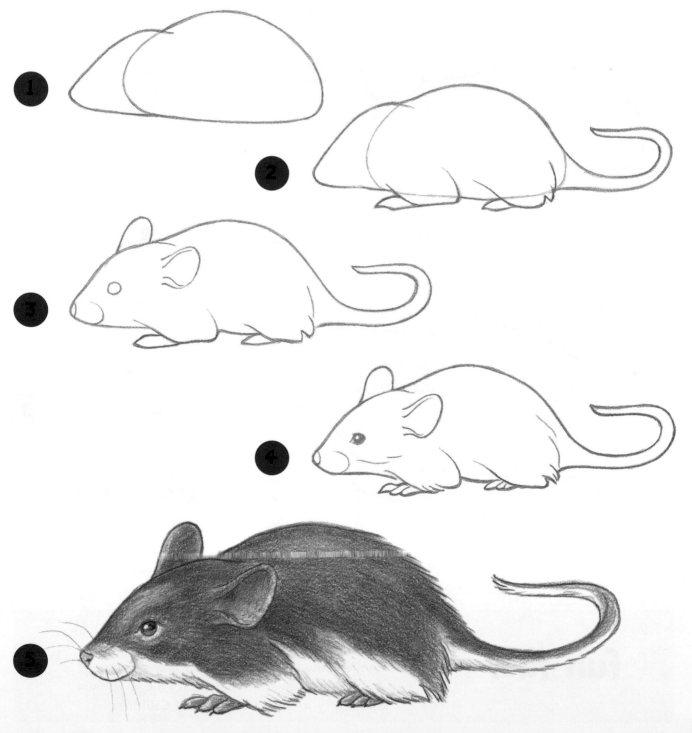

Ferret

With its slim body and small head, the ferret looks similar to a cat! But its rounded ears and masked markings distinguish it from most pets.

fun fact

Ferrets have been domesticated for even longer than cats have. Yet the approximately 8 million domestic ferrets in the United States aren't officially recognized as pets by any state government, and it's illegal to own these furry friends in the state of California!

4

5

6

Iguana

When you draw this scaly, sun-loving reptile, be sure to make its tail longer than its head and body combined!

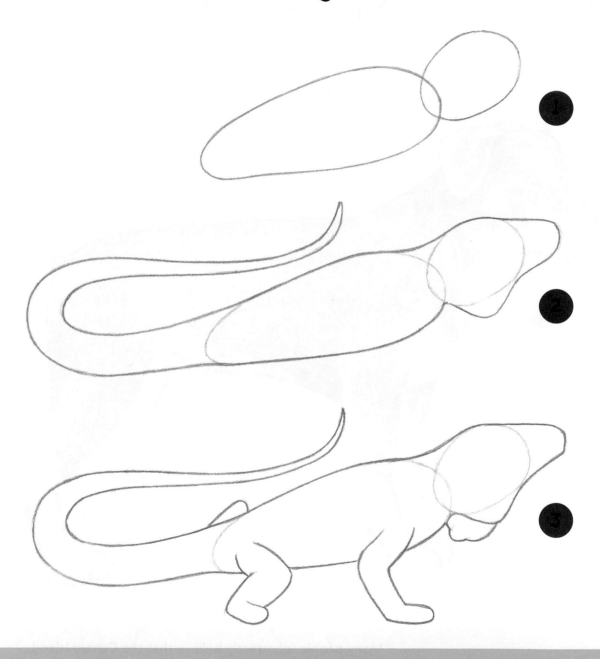

fun fact

Iguanas are a beloved pet, but they're also a popular meal in Central America! Iguana dishes are so common there that these reptiles are sometimes referred to as *gallina del palo,* or "chicken of the tree"!

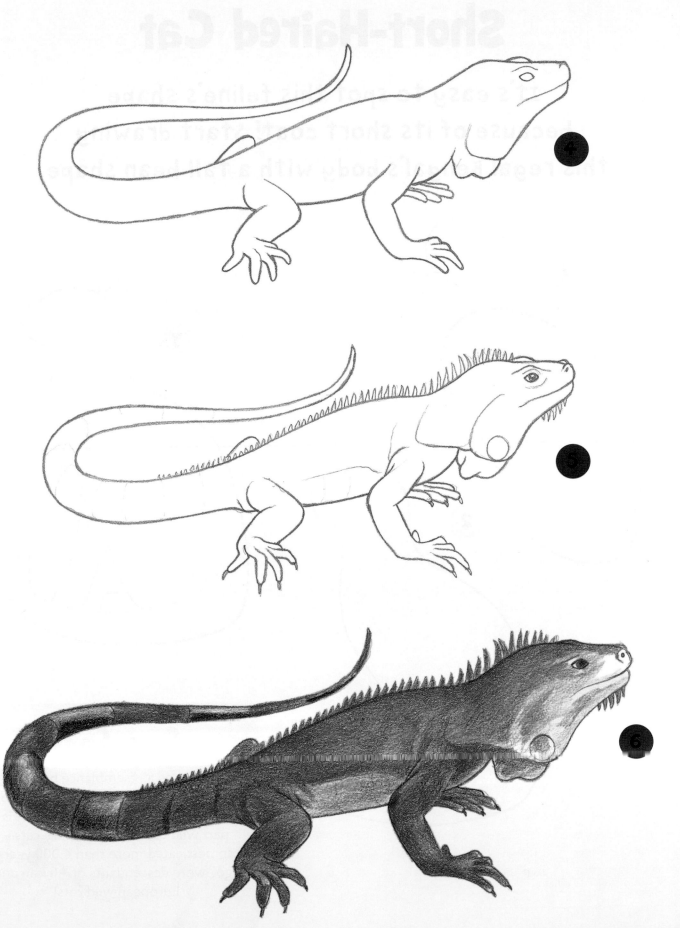

Short-Haired Cat

It's easy to spot this feline's shape because of its short coat! start drawing this regal Bengal's body with a tall bean shape.

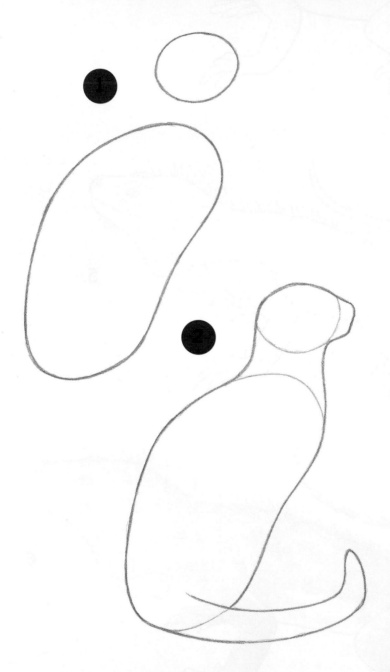

fun fact

Do you see a resemblance between your kitty and the big cats at the zoo? It may be because your house cat is part wild cat. The first house cats—domesticated more than 4,000 years ago—were descendants of African and European wild cats!

Parakeets

This pair of parakeets starts out
with similar shapes, but the birds aren't identical.
Look for the differences as you draw.

Goldfish

Drawing this goldfish is as simple as can be!
Begin with an egg shape for the body,
and then add the flowing fins!

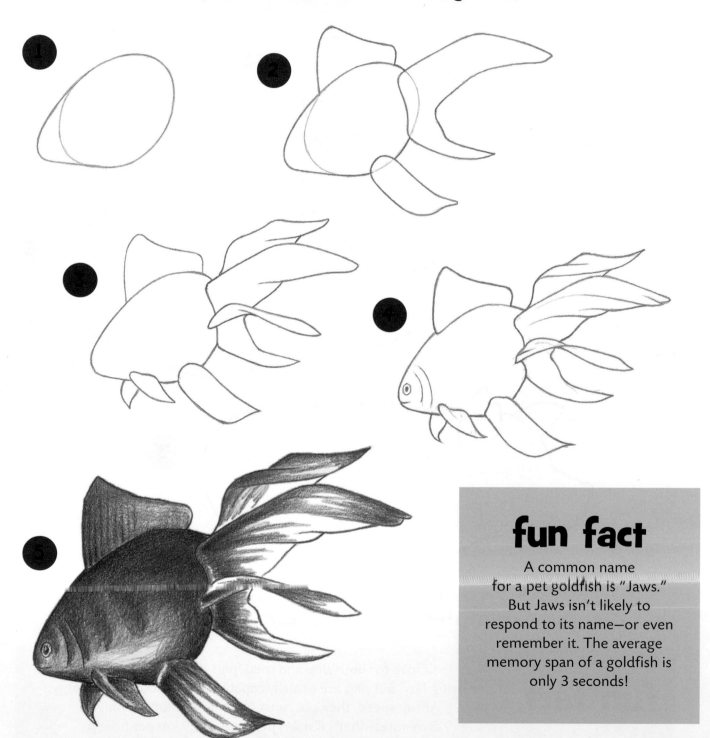

fun fact

A common name
for a pet goldfish is "Jaws."
But Jaws isn't likely to
respond to its name—or even
remember it. The average
memory span of a goldfish is
only 3 seconds!

Pot-Bellied Pig

"Porkers" like this one love to pig out, so it's no surprise that this swine's hallmark feature is its big round belly.

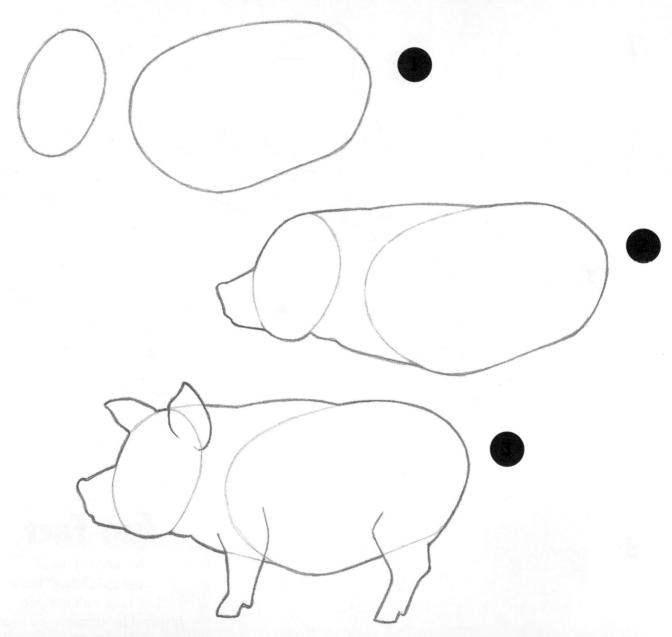

fun fact

With their love for both slop and mud, pigs have gained a reputation for being lazy. But pigs are actually capable of great bursts of energy. At top speed, they can run a full mile (1.6 km) in only 7.5 minutes—that's 8 miles per hour (12.9 km per hour)!

Snake

S-s-s-start with two oval shapes to snake yourself into position to draw this slithery coiled Python.

Hermit Crab

The hermit crab's shell once belonged to a sea snail or other ocean creature. Hermit crabs find empty shells and move into them for protection.

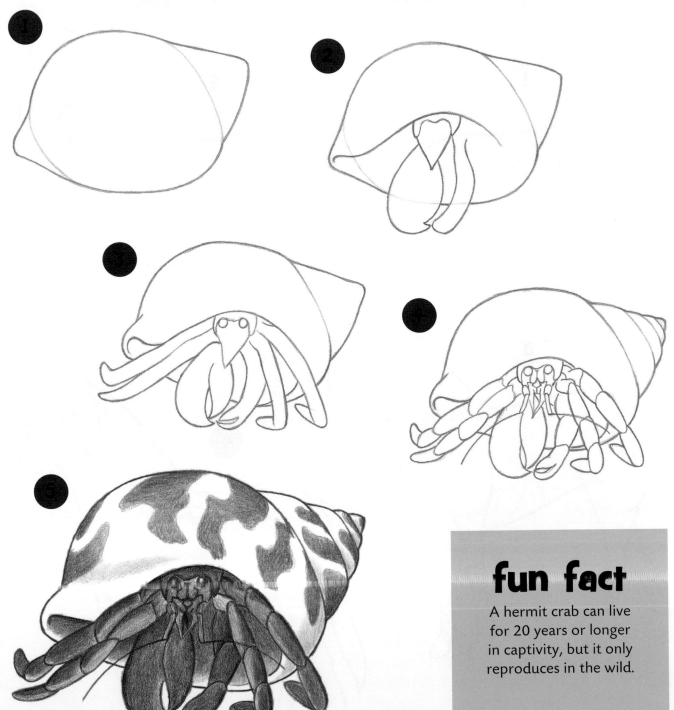

fun fact

A hermit crab can live for 20 years or longer in captivity, but it only reproduces in the wild.

Pony

Ponies are shorter than horses, but they're usually stronger! Draw this pet with a thick body and muscular legs.

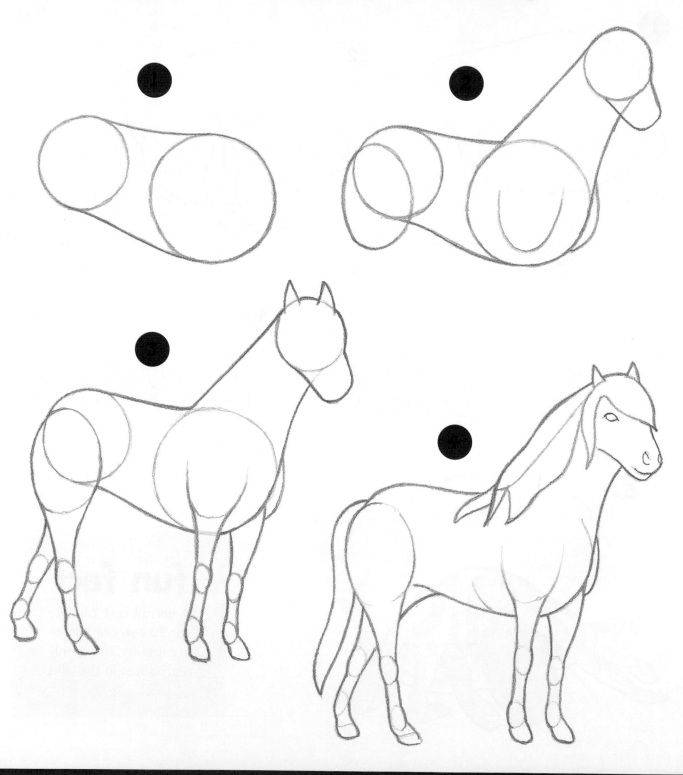

5

6

Tarantula

An Arachnid is a different kind of "furry" friend! This spider has eight shaggy legs and two shorter "arms" in front of its body.

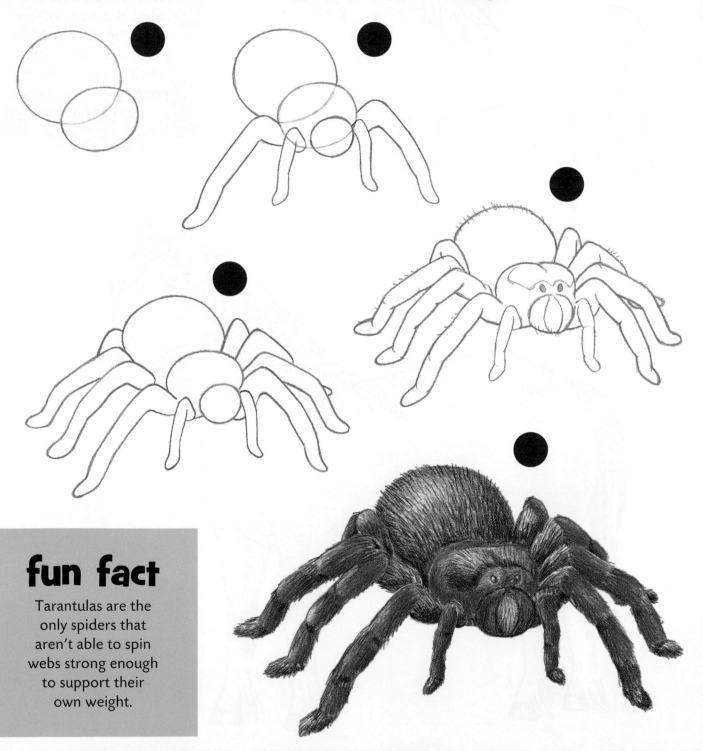

fun fact

Tarantulas are the only spiders that aren't able to spin webs strong enough to support their own weight.

Tortoise

This shell-back moves slowly because it takes its home wherever it goes! Its four thick, strong legs have to work hard.

Guinea Pig

This little cowlicked fur ball is more closely related to a mouse than to a pig. It may be the only pet with permanent "bedhead"!

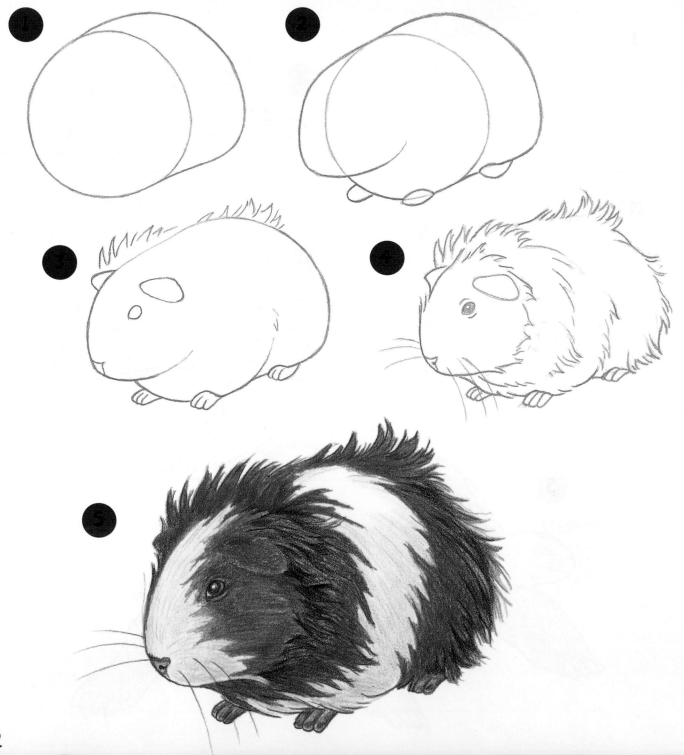